Personal evolution series

Factuality

The divine order

Mind over matter

Spiritually connected

Surviving our lowest point

For the love of pets

Lucifer's revenge

Karma sutra from a master seducer

Seven times the deadly sinner

Business is business no skin color required

Guardian the ghetto hero

From legends to legacy

Flawless potential

Pets everyday training solutions

Street style

The power within

The evolution of discrimination

Unspoken reality

Gang eighty-fifth

Sacrificed by sins

Rider evolution

John lee love's pro flatlander b.m.x

Love

Televised persuasion

Forced by any means necessary

The 7 keys of success

JOHN LEE LOVE'S
PRO FLATLANDER
B.M.X

A Step By Step Guide To Mastering My Personal (Top 7) B.M.X Flatland Tricks

By John L. Love

JOHN LEE LOVE'S PRO FLATLANDER B.M.X

Copyright © 2020 by John Lee Love

All rights reserved. Except for use in any review, the reproduction or utilization of this work in whole or part in any form by any electronic, mechanical, or other means, now known or hereafter invented, including xerography, photocopying, and recording, or in any information storage or retrieval system, is forbidden without the permission of the copyright holder.

The characters in this book are based on Nonfictional characters, including the information & its original contents which are based on Nonfictional events.

Printed in the U.S.A

June 2020

By John Lee Love

AUTHOR QOUTE

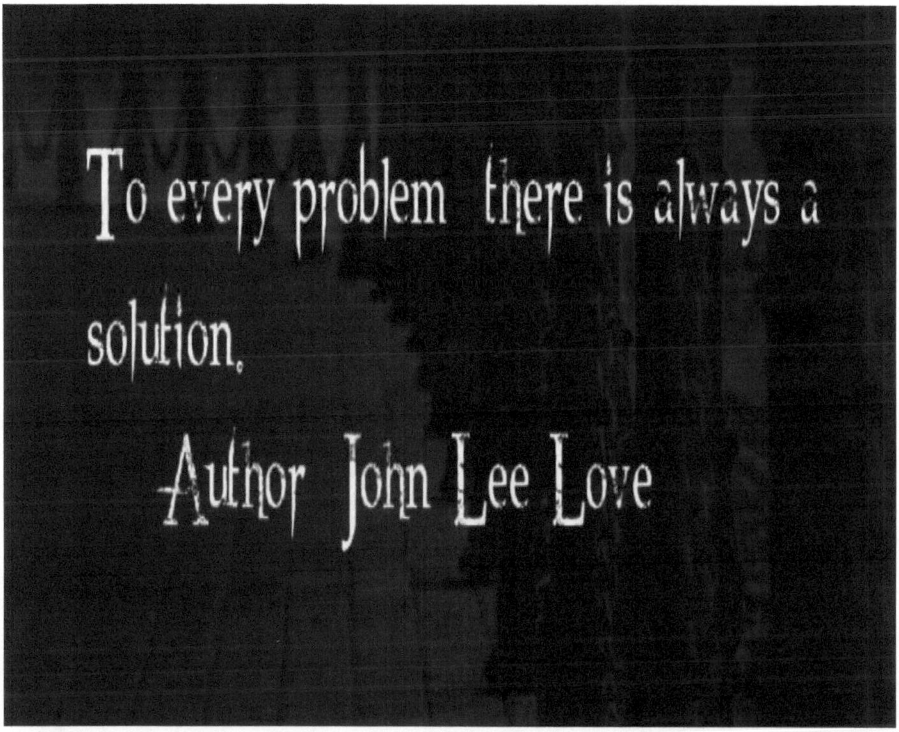

To every problem there is always a solution.

Author John Lee Love

Flatland, Freestyle, or Vert!

When it comes to **B.M.X**, learning the tricks can take lots of time; but mostly balance. Balance is <u>**ALWAYS**</u> key to ***mastering ALL*** the different styles of tricks to B.M.X

No-matter your style, no-matter your height, or weight. Mastering your balance will save you the time it would take someone who doesn't know their own balance.

Know this, master it, then share the love!!!

Table Of Contents

Hydration First!

When it comes to learning (**ANYTHING PHYSICAL**).

Always remember your bodies (**Hydration**) levels. Knowing how hydrated you are, will always keep you going at rates, only your body can handle. Whenever I practice, even at my current age in this photo (**34yrs**), I drink multiple bottles of **water daily**!

Just to keep me going for the hours to get things done, even if it's not practicing.

Mastering Your Balance

Body Balance Mastery is a (**Time**) consuming skill.

Any-type of riding style you may choose, will always need (**precise**) balance. This balance needs to be mastered; **BEFORE** you get on your bike to perform **ANY** tricks of any-kind!

STEPS TO PERFORM

THE

SUPER-SURF

First, start off by riding your bike; like how you see here, (**Normal**) position.

Then, proceed to stand on the (**Body**) bar of the bike, like shown here. only do this with your (**Less**) <u>**dominant leg**</u>!!!

While doing this, take your (**Balancing**) leg to stand on the (**Handle-bars**). This leg controls & steers your bikes <u>**front-end**</u>.

Lastly, (**Release**) your hands **slowly** as you find your balance point; while riding.

Once found, slowly lift your body (**Up**) with your arms outward; so that you keep the bike, **upright**, & **NOT** slanted.... like as you see here in this image.

To (**End**) the trick, just **reverse** your steps. Slowly keep a steady balance, while lowering your body back down. Then grab the handle-bars & put your feet back onto your bike peddles.

STEPS TO PERFORM

THE

FRONT-WHEEL REVERSE-DRIVE

&

GHOST-RIDE THE WHIP

First, start off by riding your bike; like how you see here, (**climb-over**) position.

While climbing over the handle-bars; place your balancing (**Foot**) on one of your (**Pegs**) to balance your bike, while **shifting** your (**Body-Weight**) to keep your bike from **tilting**. Do this to climb-over your handle-bars.

Once over the handle-bars, keep your body (**Off**) the handle-bars. This will allow you to keep balance; **<u>without</u>** making your bike tilt (**forward**), or **<u>sideways</u>**. While in this position, use your balancing leg to (**Kick-off**) the front-wheel; this will allow your bike to keep **<u>rolling</u>** without **<u>falling</u>**.

Lastly, to end the trick, just reverse your steps. Start-off with balancing your bike; while (still) performing the trick, & do a (Backwards) kick to get your leg back (over) the handle-bars. Use this same leg to land its foot on your bikes (body) pole; which will allow your other leg to make its way back to your bike peddles, when you fill comfortable to do so.

STEPS TO PERFORM

THE

BLINDMAN'S STUNT

First, start off by riding your bike; like how you see here, (**Backwards**) position.

Then, (**slowly**) put <u>one</u> foot onto the (**Body**) frame of your bike. Next, put your (**Dominant**) foot onto the handlebars.

Next, (**slowly**) release your hand from the handlebars & raise your body (**back-side**) as high as you can get it into the air; while staying in that pose. Make sure you watch your surroundings to make sure you don't crash.

Lastly, to end the trick, simply **<u>reverse</u>** your steps. Do this by slowly climbing back down the handlebars; like you see here in this image of me.

STEPS TO PERFORM

THE

SUICIDE-NOSEDIVE

First, start off by riding your bike; like how you see here, (**Backwards**) position.

Next, proceed climbing up the handlebars, with your (**dominant**) foot planted on the (**Body**) bar of your bike-frame.

Use your (**Non-Dominant**) leg as high as you can while tilting your body **up-side-down**; while holding your handlebars. Keep your body very still as possible, while **focusing your vision** slightly behind yourself. Do this to avoid crashes.

Lastly, to end the trick, just do the steps in **reverse**. Slowly bring your leg back down from being in the air; & back onto your bike as shown in the image below.

STEPS TO PERFORM

THE

REVERSE-DRIVE

First, start off by riding your bike; like how you see here (**Backwards**) Position.

Then, while riding (**Backwards**). Slowly, find your balance to slightly turn your body. Do this at a steady slow, but **medium speed**. While performing this trick, you must position your (**Butt**) on the handlebars, so you can start to see **in-front** of you; while **sitting sideways**, like you see in the image above.

Next, find a good **grabbing** (**Spot**) on your handlebars. This will allow you to continue holding your balance; while **fully turning your body** in the **frontward** position. Remember to also keep your weight adjusted with your bike, to **maintain your balance,** so your bike **doesn't** tilt.

Lastly, to end the trick, just do the steps in reverse. Just make sure you keep your balance steady, while reversing **<u>ANY</u>** trick; **<u>especially this one</u>**. It's quite simple, but can still cause you to **crash** in a **<u>painful way</u>**.

STEPS TO PERFORM

THE

STREET-SWEEPER

First, start off by riding your bike; like how you see here, (**Forward**) Position.

Then, **(Shift)** your body; to <u>**ANY**</u> side of your bike; whichever side feels comfortable. The side you stand on, should be your <u>**dominant hand**</u> side to help control your steering, as well as your balance.

Next, **make sure** you have (**one**) foot on your **back peg**, & the other foot still on your bike peddle. While standing like this, also **make sure** you have (**one**) hand pushing down on your bike seat, & the other **controlling your steering** on your handlebars; while **staying as close** to the ground as possible, **without** scraping the ground.

Lastly, allow your bike to (**Softly**) come to a complete stop. To end the trick, just reverse your steps; but stay in that (**Body**) position like I am in this image below. Once your bike is stopped, lift your bike, & position your body back on it to its original position.

MEET THE AUTHOR

(John Lee Love) is Author of 27 different publications including this one, in which 19 of them are self-help guides for making everyday life even better.

He is also creator & founder of (PERSONAL EVOLUTION™) his teaching brand that teaches throughout his books as well as his (YOUTUBE) channel.

In addition to this, he is also a master (Bio-Mechanics) weaponry inventor who utilizes fusion in advancing human life with products that helps us live better without the use of medications. He currently resides in Minneapolis Minnesota with his family.

www.ingramcontent.com/pod-product-compliance
Lightning Source LLC
Chambersburg PA
CBHW040932110726
48006CB00001B/154